W9-BJP-542

ELEMENTARY
SCHOOL LIBRARY

ELEPHANTS

by Cynthia Overbeck

Photographs by Tokumitsu Iwago

A Lerner Natural Science Book

Lerner Publications Company ▪ Minneapolis

Sylvia A. Johnson, Series Editor

Translation by Setsuko Takeuchi
Additional research by Jane Dallinger

LIBRARY OF CONGRESS CATALOGING IN PUBLICATION DATA

Overbeck, Cynthia.
  Elephants.

    (A Lerner natural science book)
    Adapted from The world of wild elephants by T.
  Iwagō, originally published under title: Yasei zō no
  sekai.
    Includes index.
    SUMMARY: Discusses the largest land animal on
  earth, which now lives only in Africa and Asia.

    1. Elephants—Juvenile literature. [1. Elephants]
  I. Iwagō, Tokumitsu. II. Iwagō, Tokumitsu. Yasei zō
  no sekai. English. III. Title. IV. Series: Lerner natural
  science book.

  QL737.P98093   599.6'1   80-27550
  ISBN 0-8225-1452-4

This edition first published 1981 by Lerner Publications Company.
Revised text copyright © 1981 by Lerner Publications Company.
Photographs copyright © 1972 by Tokumitsu Iwago.
Adapted from THE WORLD OF WILD ELEPHANTS copyright © 1972
by Tokumitsu Iwago. English language rights arranged by
Japan UNI Agency, Inc. for Akane Shobo Publishers, Tokyo.

All rights reserved. International copyright secured.
Manufactured in the United States of America.

International Standard Book Number: 0-8225-1452-4
Library of Congress Catalog Card Number: 80-27550

    4 5 6 7 8 9 10 90 89 88 87

A Note on Scientific Classification

The animals in this book are sometimes called by their scientific names as well as by their common English names. These scientific names are part of the system of **classification**, which is used by scientists all over the world. Classification is a method of showing how different animals (and plants) are related to each other. Animals that are alike are grouped together and given the same scientific name.

Those animals that are very much like one another belong to the same **species** (SPEE-sheez). This is the basic group in the system of classification. An animal's species name is made up of two words in Latin or Greek. For example, the species name of the lion is *Panthera leo*. This scientific name is the same in all parts of the world, even though an animal may have many different common names.

The next group in scientific classification is the **genus** (GEE-nus). A genus is made up of more than one species. Animals that belong to the same genus are closely related but are not as much alike as the members of the same species. The lion belongs to the genus *Panthera*, along with its close relatives the leopard, *Panthera pardus*, the tiger, *Panthera tigris*, and the jaguar, *Panthera onca*. As you can see, the first part of the species name identifies the animal's genus.

Just as a genus is made up of several species, a **family** is made up of more than one genus. Animals that belong to the same family are generally similar but have some important differences. Lions, leopards, tigers, and jaguars all belong to the family Felidae, a group that also includes cheetahs and domestic cats.

Families of animals are parts of even larger groups in the system of classification. This system is a useful tool both for scientists and for people who want to learn about the world of nature.

On the grassy plains of Africa and in the dense forests of Asia lives the biggest land animal on earth—the elephant. A full-grown elephant can tower as high as 13 feet (3.9 meters). It may weigh up to 14,000 pounds (6,350 kilograms). This means that it is almost as heavy as an entire school bus!

These huge animals once wandered over many parts of the world. The ancestors of today's elephants first appeared in Africa in prehistoric times. From Africa they spread through Europe, Asia, and North and South America.

Today, however, wild elephants are found in only a few parts of Africa and southern Asia. These places have just the right environment to support elephant life.

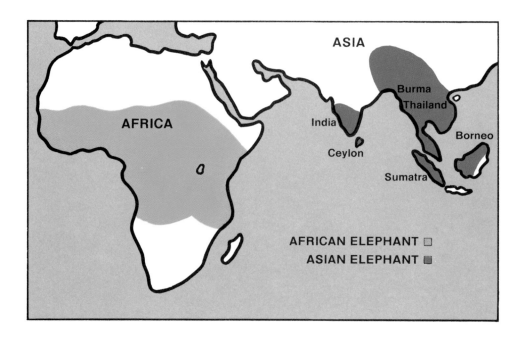

If they have to, elephants can survive in many different kinds of environments. They can live in cool mountain regions or in dry, desert-like areas. But they live best in places that have warm temperatures and plenty of rainfall. In these areas there are large amounts of grasses, bushes, and trees, which elephants need for food and shade.

Once there were many different species of elephants. But today there are only two. *Loxodonta africana* is the African elephant. It lives on the **savannas*** (suh-VAN-nahs), or grassy plains, of Central and South Africa. *Elephas maximus* is the Asian or Indian elephant. It lives in the forests of India, Thailand, and other countries of Southeast Asia.

*Words in **bold type** are defined in the glossary at the end of the book.

6

The African elephant roams the savannas.

The Asian elephant in its forest environment

The African elephant   The Asian elephant

There are several ways in which the African elephant looks different from its Asian cousin. First, the African elephant is larger. An average adult male stands about 11½ feet (3.5 meters) tall. The Asian male is usually about 9 feet (2.7 meters) tall. The females of both species are smaller than the males. Both male and female African elephants have tusks on either side of their trunks. But Asian females, and some males, have no tusks at all. The African elephant's ears are huge and fanlike—larger than those of the Asian elephant. Its head is fairly flat, and there is a slight hollow in the middle of its back. The Asian elephant has a humped back and two round bumps on its head. Finally, the African elephant's skin is a darker gray than that of the Asian elephant.

Except for these differences, the bodies of African and Asian elephants are very much the same. The most unusual part of an elephant's body is its trunk. With its strong, flexible trunk, an elephant can do a surprising variety of jobs. An elephant's trunk can even do some of the things that a human hand can do.

First of all, the elephant's trunk is its nose, and it does the same work as the noses of other animals. The nostrils, or openings through which air passes, are in the tip of the trunk. Elephants have a good sense of smell. They will often raise their trunks high in the air to pick up an interesting scent.

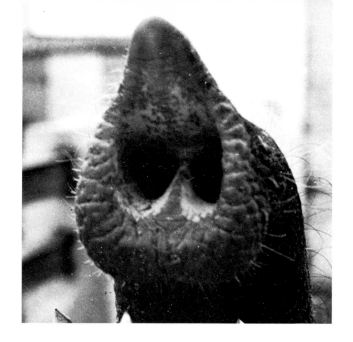

An elephant also uses its trunk as a tool for doing various jobs. The trunk is made mostly of muscle. It is very, very strong. With it, the elephant can pick up objects that weigh as much as 600 pounds (270 kilograms). This powerful "arm" is also used to beat off attacking animals. Sometimes mother elephants even use their trunks (more gently, of course) to "spank" their babies!

Not only is the elephant's trunk strong, but it is also flexible. This means that it can bend, curl, and move around easily. The trunk can roll back up over the elephant's forehead. Or it can curl under toward the animal's mouth. It can move from side to side, too. At the end of the trunk are two "lips." (The Asian elephant has only one.) These are used almost like a human thumb and finger to grasp small objects.

This ability comes in handy when the elephant is hungry. The elephant picks up some fruit with the tip of its trunk. Or it wraps its whole trunk around a large bunch of leaves. Then it curls its trunk under and stuffs the food into its mouth.

Elephants also use their trunks to drink water. An elephant can suck up to 2 gallons (7.6 liters) of water into its trunk at once. A thirsty elephant fills its trunk at the waterhole. Then it squirts the water into its mouth. On hot afternoons, the elephant uses its trunk to give itself a shower.

Finally, elephants use their trunks to communicate. They make a great many noises. They make a loud, shrill sound, called **trumpeting**, to frighten an enemy. They also make noises to call for help or just to keep in touch with each other.

An elephant uses its trunk to give itself a shower.

Besides their useful trunks, some elephants have **tusks** that help them to do certain jobs. These tusks are actually the elephants' front teeth, or **incisors** (in-SI-zors). They keep on growing throughout the animals' lives. A male African elephant's tusks can grow to be as long as 11½ feet (3.5 meters). They can weigh up to 235 pounds (105.8 kilograms). The tusks are made of a hard white material called **ivory**. They are very strong. Elephants often use their tusks to dig roots out of the ground for food. The pointed ends of the tusks are useful weapons during a fight, too.

In addition to the teeth that grow into tusks, an elephant has four big teeth called **molars**. These molars can be quite large —up to a foot (30 cm) wide. They are inside the elephant's mouth and are used for chewing and grinding food.

Elephants lose their teeth and grow new ones, just like people do. But while a person loses his or her teeth only once, an elephant gets *six* new sets of molars in a lifetime. As one set of molars wears out, a new set grows in behind it. Eventually, the old ones fall out.

The elephant gets its last set of molars when it is about 40 years old. When this set wears out, the elephant can no longer chew its food. By the age of 60 or 70 years, most elephants finally starve to death.

Elephants use their sharp tusks as weapons and as tools to dig roots out of the ground.

When an African elephant is angry or frightened, its big ears stand out from the sides of its head.

Another unusual part of the elephant's body are its huge ears, which can be as wide as 4 feet (1.2 meters) in male African elephants. These enormous ears have many purposes. Since elephants have poor eyesight, the animals depend on their sense of hearing, as well as smell, to warn them of danger. When an elephant senses that an enemy is near, it holds its huge ears straight out from the sides of its head. This makes the elephant look especially big and frightening.

Elephants can hear danger coming, and they can also use their big ears to scare enemies away. The elephant's ears have even more uses. When an elephant is resting or eating, it flaps its ears to keep bothersome insects away. And on hot afternoons, elephants cool themselves by fanning their ears constantly. This action cools off the blood in the ears themselves. The cooled blood then moves through the animal's system and lowers the temperature in the rest of its body.

All of these special body features help an elephant to live comfortably in its natural environment. The way in which elephants live together as a group also helps them to survive.

Elephants live in family groups. The females, or **cows,** are the real centers of the families. A mother elephant and 2 to 5 of her babies, called **calves**, form the main family group. The adult males, called **bulls**, are not a permanent part of the family. They stay with one cow for a short time in order to mate. But they are independent the rest of the time.

Sometimes, however, the bulls band together with other bulls and many families to form a herd. Elephants form herds to help and protect each other when they are traveling from one place to another in search of food and water. Usually, a herd will stay together for only a short time.

Right: A mother elephant and her calf. Female elephants have calves only about once every four years.

A typical herd is made up of 20 to 50 elephants, but herds of 500 or more have been known to form. Generally one of the older cows leads the herd. The members of a herd act as a real community. They take care of one another. The strong adults help weaker members—the old, the sick, and the calves.

When a new calf is born, the whole herd gets in on the act. All the elephants form a circle around the mother to keep her safe. One cow, called an "auntie," gives the mother special help. Once the calf is born, it must learn to stand up right away. The auntie and other cows and calves try to help the new calf stand up. They nudge and support it with their trunks. After a while, the herd moves back and the calf stands up.

A newborn calf is very weak. It is also small—for an elephant. It is about 3 feet (.9 meters) tall and weighs about 200 pounds (90 kilograms). For the first few days of its life, it stays under its mother's belly. There it can suck milk from her breasts, which are between her front legs. The calf does not use its trunk to suck the milk. Instead, it curls its trunk back over its head and sucks with its mouth. The calf will drink its mother's milk until it is about two years old. Then it will begin learning to eat and drink on its own.

The young elephant calves are carefully protected by the adults in the herd. If an enemy comes near, the calves form a circle together with the cows. The bulls make another circle around the outside of the group. Their mighty tusks and trunks face outward, toward the enemy, and their ears stand out wide on either side of their heads. The bulls stamp the ground with their huge feet and trumpet loudly. Only the most determined attacker will try to break through this wall of heavy tusks and feet to reach the calves.

Though bull elephants often defend the cows and calves in this way, the cows can be just as fierce when defending their babies. Sometimes a cow and her calf may be feeding together some distance away from the herd. If an enemy tries to attack the calf, the mother will not hesitate to fight. She will smash the enemy with her trunk and trample it under her feet.

Bulls form a circle to protect the cows and calves.

All the adults are especially careful to watch over the calves when the herd is on the move from one feeding ground to another. The adults help the calves over rough parts of the trail. They use their trunks and tusks to push and pull the calves. Often a herd must climb in or out of a deep ditch. The adults may then stamp special steps into the sides of the ditch for the calves to use.

Elephants also help the sick and old adults in the herd. Often, a young elephant will stay with an older one, helping it and protecting it. Sometimes, two healthy adults will come

up on either side of a sick elephant and hold it up. If an old or sick elephant cannot get up, the herd will form a circle around it to protect it.

Elephants are very clever at figuring out how to help weaker members of the herd. There are many stories about how elephants help each other. For example, they have been known to free a fellow elephant that is stuck in deep mud. A herd of elephants may work for hours to stamp out a firm piece of ground around the muddy area. Then they push the trapped animal onto the firm ground.

Besides helping each other out, elephants often behave very affectionately toward one another. When two elephants meet, they touch trunks or rub shoulders. Sometimes two elephants will even put the tips of their trunks together, almost as if they are kissing. Or they will just stand still, close to each other, for a long time.

While most elephants stay in groups, some old or sick elephants go off alone. If these animals are in pain from sickness or wounds, they sometimes go crazy. They blindly attack anything or anyone in their path. Such dangerous loners are called **rogues** (ROHGS).

Generally, however, elephants stay together in herds. They move about a great deal in their constant search for food and water. These huge animals need enormous amounts of food. An adult elephant eats up to 600 pounds (270 kilograms) of grass and leaves daily. When there is plenty of water to be found, elephants can drink up to 40 gallons (152 liters) of water in a day. It's easy to see why elephants need to travel around from place to place. If they stayed in one spot, they would soon strip all the trees and bushes bare of leaves. There would be nothing left for them to eat.

The distance that a herd travels in one day changes with the seasons. In the rainy season, there is usually a good supply of leaves and grasses throughout the countryside. Then, a herd will range from 8 to 20 miles (12.8 to 32 kilometers) in a day, eating constantly. When the land is dry, the herd will march as far as 30 miles (48 kilometers) a day in search of food and water.

The herd moves slowly, babies in the rear. The adults can walk about 8 miles per hour (12.8 kmph). For short distances, they can run up to 25 miles per hour (40 kmph). But usually they move about 6 miles per hour (9.6 kmph). The herd passes through a wide and varied countryside as it travels. Often the elephants must cross rivers in their journey. If the river isn't too deep, they simply walk across. They will even walk across the river bottom when the water is over their heads. They just put their trunks up above the water, like snorkels, to breathe. In very deep rivers, where their feet cannot touch the bottom, the elephants swim across. Despite their size, they are very good swimmers.

When the herd reaches a place where there is plenty of

WALKERTON ELEMENTARY
SCHOOL LIBRARY

water, the elephants may stay there for a while. They use the lake or river as a home base. From there, they wander off each day to look for food.

Elephants are always hungry, and they eat almost all the time. Elephants are **herbivores** (ER-bih-vorz), which means that they eat no meat. Their diet consists of roots, grasses, leaves, tree branches, and even tree bark. A herd of hungry elephants can do a lot of damage to trees in their feeding area. They use their tusks to rip the bark off the trees. Sometimes they knock down whole trees! They ram the trees with their foreheads until the trees topple over. Then the elephants eat the tender leaves that grow at the treetops. An elephant's idea of a real treat is fruit. Elephants love to eat bananas, mangoes, berries, and coconuts.

Elephants do much of their eating at night, when the air is coolest. In the daytime, when it is very hot, they sleep about four or five hours. They spend a lot of time in the shade or by the waterhole. To stay cool, they may give themselves a shower with their trunks. Or they may take a mud bath. They do this by sucking wet mud into their trunks and spraying it over their bodies. Mud baths also help to protect their skin from biting insects.

**This elephant
is spraying itself
with sand.**

An elephant's skin is tough. It is about an inch (2.5 cm) thick! In fact, one term for an elephant—**pachyderm** (PAK-ih-durm)—means "thick-skinned." As thick as it is, however, the elephant's skin is very tender in places. That is why the elephant sometimes needs a cool layer of mud on its skin to keep insects from biting.

Sometimes, elephants also take dry sand up into their trunks and spray the sand over themselves. They probably do this for fun rather than for any useful purpose.

Except for pesky insects, elephants share their waterholes and riverbanks peacefully with birds and other animals. Few animals attack the huge adult elephants. Sometimes, however, tigers, lions, leopards, or hyenas will try to kill the elephant calves for food.

White egrets walk fearlessly around this elephant's feet,
looking for insects to eat.

A tiger, for example, may find a mother alone with a calf, away from the rest of the herd. The tiger will jump on the mother's back and claw her. Sometimes, the mother runs away in fright. Then the tiger comes back and kills the calf. But at other times the tiger is the loser. It is thrown to the ground and trampled by the mother and by other elephants that come to the rescue.

Small animals can also cause trouble for an elephant. You may have heard that elephants are afraid of mice. This isn't exactly true. But mice and other small animals can cause special problems for the elephant. Sometimes a mouse runs up inside an elephant's trunk. Then the elephant goes wild. It sucks up water to blow out the creature, or it beats its trunk against a tree over and over again. Elephants can hurt themselves badly when they do this.

While some small animals cause trouble for the elephant, one creature—the egret—is very helpful to its giant friend. This fearless bird rides on the elephant's back or hops around in the grass near its huge feet. It eats ticks and insects that land on the elephant's skin. It also eats the grasshoppers and other insects that hop out of the grass when the elephant walks by. Sometimes a group of egrets will fly around an elephant and bother it so that it will move and stir up more insects. In turn, the birds provide a sort of warning system for the elephant. If any enemies are nearby, the egrets become frightened. They fly up, calling out loudly. This warns the elephant that danger is near.

Two young elephants follow an adult across a road.

The most dangerous of the elephant's enemies are not tigers or any other wild animals. They are people. Because of human beings, there are fewer and fewer elephants left roaming wild in the world. In the past, many people killed elephants just for their tusks. The ivory of which the tusks are made is a valuable material because it is both beautiful and rare. It is made into carvings and jewelry. It is also used to make piano keys.

People have also reduced the number of elephants by taking over land once used by the elephants. As we have seen, the elephants' huge appetites cause them to travel over great distances to find food. The crops of the farmers in Africa and Asia provide a ready-made meal for a hungry herd of elephants. Farmers can't build fences or buildings strong enough to keep the huge animals out.

The farmers and their families need the crops that grow in order to survive. So they often kill or capture elephants that raid their fields, gardens, or storerooms. With less and less room to roam and find food, the elephants that are left may starve to death.

In Africa and Asia, special **reserves** have been set up to protect elephants from people, and vice versa. Such reserves include Kenya's Royal Tsavo National Park and Uganda's Queen Elizabeth National Park, both in Africa. These are huge fenced parks, or outdoor zoos, acres and acres in size. They preserve the elephants' natural environment. Within their fences, elephants and other wild animals can roam freely. Tourists can drive through the reserves and look at the animals from the safety of their cars.

Hunters are not allowed to kill elephants or other animals on these reserves. In turn, the reserves also protect people from the elephants. The elephants cannot get out to eat the crops that people need to live.

Such reserves should protect the elephants, but sadly some people disobey the laws governing the reserves. These people, called **poachers**, kill the animals in spite of the laws.

Most of the elephants of Africa roam freely on reserves. Because the adults are very dangerous, people have never really attempted to tame them.

In Asia, there are only about 200 wild elephants, all of them living in Gir Sanctuary, a forest reserve in India. Most Asian elephants are tame animals kept by the people of India and Southeast Asia. The Asian elephant is intelligent and has a gentle temperament. This makes it easy to tame and to train. These elephants are trained to do useful work for people in remote areas of India and many Southeast Asian lands. Here, in dense forests and undeveloped areas, trucks and other vehicles are hard to use. Instead, elephants often carry people and goods from one place to another.

Elephants are especially useful in the highland teak forests of Asia. This is where teak trees are cut by the logging industry. Elephants are trained to carry heavy teak logs on their tusks. They carry them down the mountain sides to the riverbanks below. There they put the logs in the river. The logs float downstream to the lumber mills. At the mills, other elephants take the logs out of the water. They "feed" the logs to a large saw, which cuts the logs into boards. Then the elephants stack the cut boards in neat piles.

An elephant will not be expected to handle really heavy work like this until it is about 20 years old. But the elephant's training begins when it reaches the age of five. The elephant is paired with one special worker. The two may stay together as a team for their entire lives. The worker teaches the animal 20 to 30 different voice commands. The worker also gives the elephant orders by touching it in a certain way on the ears, neck, and trunk. Often the worker rides on the elephant's back as it does its work.

Both the human and the elephant work hard at their jobs. They begin work very early in the day, during the cool hours. They rest during the mid-day heat. Then they work again into the evening.

At the end of the long workday, the tired elephant is taken down to the river. There, it gets a well-earned bath in the cool water. The worker scrubs the exhausted animal from head to toe.

In addition to logging work, elephants in the countries of Southeast Asia are given lighter jobs to do. They are often used in ceremonies and religious festivals. There, they carry important people in parades. These elephants are painted with gaily colored flowers. They wear fancy gold trappings and rich-colored cloths.

In Western countries such as the United States, Canada, and the European nations, Asian elephants are often seen in circuses. They are given special training so that they can do all kinds of tricks. They can stand on two legs or balance on a large ball. Circus elephants have been favorites of children for many years.

Today, circus elephants and those kept in zoos are the only ones that most people ever see. Not many of us have the opportunity to watch wild elephants on the reserves in Africa and Asia. But at least we know that in these protected areas there are elephants living a free and natural life. On the African savannas and in the Indian forest, that amazing animal the elephant continues to survive.

GLOSSARY

bull—a male elephant

calf—a baby elephant

cow—a female elephant

herbivore—an animal that eats only plants, and no meat

incisors—sharp or pointed front teeth used for cutting

ivory—the hard, white material that forms the tusks of elephants and other tusked animals like the walrus

molars—flat teeth used for grinding food

pachyderm—a large, thick-skinned animal with hoofs, such as the elephant or rhinoceros

poacher—a person who hunts and kills animals illegally

reserve—a place set aside by people for animals, where the animals can live in their natural environment. In a reserve, hunting animals is against the law.

rogue—an old or sick elephant that goes off to live by itself

savanna—a tropical or subtropical grassland area with scattered trees and shrubs

trumpeting—a loud, shrill noise that elephants make when in distress or danger

tusks—long, pointed incisor teeth that extend outside of an animal's mouth

INDEX

African elephant, 6, 9, 10,
    14, 40
Asian elephant, 6, 9, 10, 11, 40
birth of baby elephant, 20
bulls (male elephants), 19

calves (baby elephants), 19
circuses, elephants in, 44-45
communication of elephants,
    12
cows (female elephants), 19

daily activities, 27-29, 31
damage caused by elephants,
    29, 37
defenses of elephants, 22-23,
    35
development of young
    elephants, 20

ears, 17
enemies, 32, 35, 37
environment of elephants, 5-6,
    17

family life, 19, 20, 22,
    24-25, 26
food, 12, 27, 29, 31, 37

Gir Sanctuary (India), 40

herbivores, 29
herds, elephant, 19-20, 22,
    24, 27, 28

ivory, 14, 37

mating, 19

pachyderm, 32
poachers, 38

reserves, 38, 40, 45
rogues, 26

size of elephants, 5, 9

tame elephants in Asia,
    40-42
teeth, 14
trumpeting, 12
trunk, uses of, 10-12, 22-23,
    24
tusks, 9, 14, 22-23, 24, 29, 37

work done by elephants,
    40-42, 44